CROWS IN THE JUKEBOX

POEMS

MIKE JAMES

HARMONY SERIES
BOTTOM DOG PRESS
HURON, OHIO

© 2017 Bottom Dog Press
ISBN: 978-1-947504-02-8
Bottom Dog Press, Inc.
PO Box 425, Huron, OH 44839
Lsmithdog@aol.com
http://smithdocs.net
CREDITS:
General Editor: Larry Smith
Cover & Layout Design: Susanna Sharp-Schwacke
Cover Art: Heather Symmes

Some of the poems have appeared, sometimes in different versions, in the following publications:

Iodine, South Florida Poetry Journal, GTK Journal, Poetry in Plain Sight, Eunoia Review, Verse Virtual, Main Street Rag, Sanskrit, Misfit, Janus Head, Mud Season Review, Miller's Pond, Homestead Review, riverrun, Nerve Cowboy, Trailer Park Quarterly, Rusty Truck, Poem, Heneni, Orchards Poetry Journal, Cape Rock Poetry, St. Andrews Review, Wild Goose Review, Uppagus, Bathtub Gin, Philadelphia Poets, Boston Literary Magazine, Dead Snakes, Homestead Review, Town Creek Poetry, Comstock Review, and *Old Red Kimono.*

"America" was included in the anthology, *Howl, 2016* published by Prism Light Press.
"Navigating in Place" was included in the anthology, *Recession in Neverland*, published by Paladin Knight Publishing.
"Talking with Allen Ginsberg, in a Dream" was included in the anthology, *Stone River Sky*, published by Negative Capability Press.

Mike James' *Crows in the Jukebox* rises from the most human of subjects: family, memory, grief, and love. James meditates on personal, familial and communal losses and tries to make sense of the passing of time. And he does it by placing his verse in the tradition of poets such as Franz Wright, James Tate, Bill Knott, and Allen Ginsberg. These poems are honest. They rest in observation and meditation. They are lucid. Subtle. Crisp. While unadorned and unpretentious, they offer a delightfully generous and loving attention to everyday details. Along with their simple, elegant lines lies an unmistakable longing, something akin to *saudade*, a kind of melancholy for something that has not happened. Resisting sentimentality, these poems seem to nod to the end of days. They acknowledge the broken world and embody a collected sense of acceptance with a transformative sense, reminding us as James so beautifully says, "grace can come in the harvest of wild things."

—Andrea Jurjevic, author of *Small Crimes*

Reading *Crows in the Jukebox* is like driving a race car at qualifying speeds—on a track you've never driven before. There are more curves than straightaways in Mike's James's poetry, and each new turn brings surprises that are addictive.... Navigating the imagery here is one wild, imaginative ride.

—Lee Passarella, author of *Redemption*

BOTTOM DOG PRESS

TABLE OF CONTENTS

III.

IV.

I.

"Some are lucky and some are not."
—Kenneth Fearing

PHOTOGRAPH OF MY FATHER AS A YOUNG MAN

navy hadn't yet reached him
had not taken him
farther than
he would ever go again
so the hair is longer
slick and blacker from
slickness

his head tilts in mock pose
though his too rare smile
stays hidden

there's probably a coin
in his pocket
(later, always was)
for a drinker's magic trick

his shirt is neatly pressed
that never changed

the eyes don't have that distant look
we all saw later
which must have come
with family
and plans always missing
a piece

in the photograph he is thinner
somehow smaller
than he will ever seem again

After a Remark by Darrell Gray

the dark was big

we knew that as children

a field at night
          the sky stretched out
farther than
we could ever run

          still we left
our fear
beneath the porch light
with relatives

the dark was big

          an empty place to play in
imagining's storage bin

CHILDHOOD

when night was over
the stars stayed
with us

we carried them
in our coat
pockets

took them out
now and then
during
the day
watched them
light corner
shadows

they were
our compasses

though
in those days
this was years ago
we never thought
of being lost

THEORY OF FLIGHT

you walk every field for miles

never see a bush burn with
more than autumn

the sky follows you
like a habit

you try to be invisible
that never works

so you pick up every shiny rock
to wish on

the paint by numbers kit
you want for your life
never arrives

so you look for treasure
in roadside hub caps

you look for faces
in the tarnish
of wrinkled leaves

there's no cocoon
you won't crawl inside

beneath your jacket are dark wings

What's Done and Not Done

drunks lose a sense of direction
a sense of space

stairwells become narrower
steps more slanted
more uneven

top shelves of cabinets
ascend closer
to heaven's attic

if spun around
a drunken man might act like
a blindfolded child
trying to pin
a cloth tail
on a cardboard donkey

so it only makes sense
that my father
who was as much a drunk as he was anything
could forget the way back to our apartment
on hinton street

all those years of drinking must have
cost him a sense of direction

he must have had
no way to circle back

no way to walk through the door late

with apology flowers
(daisies or carnations)
and a kiss for his wife

no way to warm a sleeping son
with an extra blanket
count the son's restful breaths
hold his own

ASHES

my grandfather started smoking
when he knew he would never be rich

by the time he died, sixty years later,
(gouty and libidinous) he smoked four packs a day

sometimes, that's how it is

give up on one thing
burn away with another

it's like the sailor who grew so sick of fish
he moved to a tent in the desert

lived off cactuses and locusts
took a painted rock for his wife

he came to be known as a crazy man
in other words, a prophet

people who met him spoke of
the dark ash of his skin

the always warmth of his hands
how even his words burned

still, at night his tent became sails
the locust, seagulls

his old world, left for good on a beach,
lingered like smoke in his dreams

ON REFUSING TO SAY GRACE
BEFORE DINNER WITH MY WIFE

i don't know what to make
of the language
of grace

those words
don't cling to me
the way a blanket does
on mid-winter
mornings

or the way we cling
to one another
at night
as we swim
across the ocean of our bodies
past the edge of our wants

the night sky full of stars
mariners used
for passage
their breath filling sails
with a word
that can be a taunt
a promise
or something close to grace

home

GOING ON

rain's not worried about the slick coat
it's making for the blue jay

all day it's rained and rained
a small river taken from the sky

easy to fish for wants in a ditch
that looks like a stream

water clears away what it can
shifts part of the world to one side

it's always like this
as much as always ever is

BUILDING A BACKYARD FIRE, LATE WINTER, THINKING OF NO ONE AT ALL

my backyard fire pit hand dug, uneven,
cemented with yard rocks, re-used brick

no snow or frost though still a chill
what better time to build a fire

there's dried-out pine, scrub bush,
castoff lumber from the vacant lot next door

there's a box of matches, another of wine,
a chair and a red, wool blanket too

if my neighbor drops by we'll toast
from my box or her bottle

her last husband gone to somewhere else
since last september

the stars out in a few minutes
as of now, the sky's still blue

A PALM READING

your love line shaped less like a river
more like a wish
there are lots of scars   some
deep as trenches   encampments
from a battle   you called a draw
extra lines to trace
extra paths
your hands carry grace
and sleep   in equal measure
your life line is long
attached to a basket shaped
like regret   which is shaped like
a heart   the basket
well-made   heavy with years

TOWNSFOLK

say she can cure a wart
by touch and by curse

just let her rub her thumb
hard against the spot

let her say her words
(devil or bible wrought

she says them softly
barely more than breath)

let her ask about family
as she breaks from her task

who's related to who
by marriage and by blood

she'll ask for nothing
when she's done

offer her flowers fresh cut
fruits from a favorite tree

offer to walk her back to her farm
offer to sweep her porch clean

HOW TO FALL IN LOVE: A FOUND POEM

find the best
fresh, local
heart in
downtown

season with
wood smoke,
tears, rosemary,
age

WILD APPLES

so, here i am gathering apples
behind a neighbor's foreclosed house

andy and lauren moved away last year
the house, bank owned and empty since

over the years, this tree grew (untended,
accidental) in the corner of their acre lot

in the part of the yard they left
to weeds and shrubs and never cut

it takes at least eight years to grow a tree
so full of knotty, spotted, sour green apples

my grandfather called these horse apples
they grew wild in pastures he once knew

the fattest ones are the highest, near the sun
no horse could reach those

with my ladder and a paper grocery bag
i'll get enough for two pies

one for me and another for a neighbor
out of work, but still in her house

since sometimes dessert comes before the meal
as grace can come in the harvest of wild things

POEM

all day a crow sits on the
wooden bones of an old fence

crows are good at waiting
much better than we are
with our alphabet of wants

the crow waits for darkness
and the music it brings

darkness plays an orchestra
of self-made instruments
that crack and buzz

the one-legged cricket
masters his own jazz

SWIMMING IN THE RAIN

no lightening warns her from the river
so she swims on and on, across

the rain little more than drizzle
not as strong as the water she's in

what she knows in the water
she knows with her body

when she swims she stretches
to her full, even length

the sound of her swimming doesn't
rise above the sound of the river

if she were to cramp, cry out,
she'd not be heard or barely

still, she stays straight in her strokes
fear's only part of what's within her

when she swims she's always alone
no one who watches is with her

RED
for Ruth Bavetta

it is my favorite apple
the one i lost a first tooth on,
that streak of blood
that stained
the taste

it is the nail polish
most often
noticed

also, the background
to an old stamp
on a letter
not mailed

it's that silk robe
hung in the back
of the closet, the one
gathering dust
as it lets go of desire

First Hand Gossip

my wife tells me i was always like this
in love
with sameness
happy on the merry-go-round
at the park no one visits

even my future is repetitive

i'm the skater who endlessly loops
through two mirrored circles
one called *infinity*
the other called *again*

ONIONS

i am standing at the kitchen counter chopping
       onions
it is summer, in the early years of our marriage
we aren't yet comfortable with silence
think every moment should be filled
with laughter or lovemaking
we think this because we are young
silence is still new to us
not a friend with a hand on one shoulder
not yet the gentle indention on the couch

we fought earlier over a small purchase
pillows to make an old mattress feel half-new
now, i'm trying to think of something funny to
       say
you are in another room
folding towels in front of the television
i keep looking up from chopping during
       commercials

IN ANOTHER LIFE

he wanted to be
a desperado

like in movies
from the 1930's

whole world dusty,
black and white

he even loved the
word *desperado*

how it rhymes
with *bandelero*

how both chase
the exhale of an o

across the desert
on fast horses

past towns even
ghosts left behind

SUMMER LEGEND

that one summer
crows
gathered by hundreds
in the village

each tree
even the smallest
held more than one

their cries drowned
every sound
not
theirs

no neighbor could
remember
another summer
when they came in such
abundance

without warning
suddenly, suddenly
all of them
there

torn black blanket across the sky
one week in june

ANECDOTE IN A GRASSY FIELD

once
my old man saw a stone
suddenly decide to be a bird

the stone sprouted wings and a beak
in a quick, blinking instant
flew straight up from the ground
then away

it circled back
twice
never came down close enough
for him to catch

after a while
the stone flew past distant trees
out of sight
the whirr of wings a memory

this happened more than a while back
before i was born
when miracles took place

FRAGMENT
after Bill Knott

because always, always at least one couple is
       fighting
somewhere down a road or street
because they are mostly saying grievances
months, maybe years, old
patience, that long-winded virtue, sometimes
       gives up
after a last attempt to lecture into love, into
       submission

POEM

the man in the next house never
let us fish his pond

kept all his cold weather plenty

mother cursed him
with full breath

him and his stocked freezer

cursed his brim
his catfish   his crappie

FOR FRANZ WRIGHT
(1953-2015)

if you carried words
in a tin cup
some sparrow
would
come along
think they were
bread crumbs

you'd stand
in place
say a blessing
as he ate
the words you had left

until your body hurt
so you wished
it was no
longer yours

until your heart, quite naturally,
blossomed into wings

II.

"in fragments
like slivers of glass"
—Susan Ludvigson

SAN JOSE DEL CABO, LIKE ALWAYS

an organ grinder
in the tourist district

his dark, blue vest
shines from wear

he plays the old songs,
the old songs

here a love affair
there a loss

his tip box takes both
change and memories

as evening walkers
in shops and stalls

stop to look at what's
ready to be sold

hand-made jewelry
from re-used silver

red rope bracelets
in colored abundance

one street holds
all that's needed

down another there's
what's almost gone

AT A ROOMINGHOUSE IN NEW JERSEY
after a photograph by Simpson Kalisher

there he is beside his tea kettle and his window
the late afternoon light yellow like a faded news
        paper
he is smiling because he loves to have his
        picture taken
he is only smiling a little
he doesn't want to show too many teeth or too
        much confidence
he owns one tie and one sweater and is wearing
        both
his closet is full of smiles
he's wearing the one for this occasion
his closet door creaks like a bad violin whenever
he looks inside

THE WATCH

the day i quit the bank
still young and unafraid
david walked me
to my car
said he wanted to say goodbye
told me i had been a good friend

i barely knew him
could only say
he was single   from florida
had a rich family
collected pictures of boats
also, hummed while he ate
the lunch he brought every day

in front of my car
he shook my hand
leaned for a second on his left foot
then took his watch off
gave it to me
said

i want you to have this
this watch is worth something
will always be worth something
i have three just like it
if you are ever broke
you can pawn it
please take this
please
you should know how good a watch it is
it's swiss

STANDING NOWHERE

my wife gives me a shiny new watch
i lose it

a friend pays me a compliment
i don't know what to say

this is how it is

the compass points north
unless a magnet is nearby

the dreamer wakes throughout the night
somehow crawls back into the boat of sleep

it's possible to be draped in endlessness
look at the sky

As You Go Along
for Mbembe Milton Smith

say you make your living writing poems
that will get
people talking

let everyone know you need a bigger apartment
not only for all your books
but also for the pet goat used as a paper shredder

mention how your words come as dictation
from a muse who hides, like a prize, in your
        cereal box

talk about gold teeth as a retirement plan
and polka dots as the pattern
of the future

a beard and sunglasses are not bad for aesthetics
but nothing stands out
like an eye patch
and a willingness to speak like a pirate, now and
        then

before they take you to a quiet room
in a special hospital
for people just like you
try walking on water for at least a day

STILL LIFE, WITH SMUDGES

after tasting
one long
finger
fresh from
the yellow sun
batter of
a cake
or ladling
up the
winter taste
of venison
in stew
my grandmother
might pause
to say

*close enough
is enough*

then add
two seconds
later

*perfection's
like that
little boy
who won't
get dirty
who won't
play rough*

INSPIRATION (IN RESPONSE TO A QUESTIONNAIRE)

i don't know where it comes from
it might fall out of a dark cloud

come down heavy and biblical
a soupy mix of frogs and locusts

or (keeping in the same vein)
it might rise out of nowhere

a dust cloud
fast across the desert

or, better yet, might speak clearly
out of a dry bush, brittle as old age

there are things i need
steady as sleep

the time i spend, each day, staring
at a certain spot on the wall

my daily practice keeps a tingle
in my fingertips

keeps tension from settling
on my left shoulder too long

if i show up, stare real regular
sometimes the frogs and locusts appear

other times the spot stays a spot on the wall
now and then it becomes a bush and it calls

POEM, MOSTLY PERSONAL

i like surprises
and not just the sexual kind
either

like the time
you walked down the steps
wearing only
flip-flops
and a tuba

no, i like surprises
in general

that sudden intake
of breath

the recognition
of how the world changes
instantly
before us

the way we felt
that year in the north
when snow fell
during the richness
of summer

every red rose
dipped in
white

THE SHAPE OF THE SUN
for Heather Symmes

if i could only
paint as well
as when
i was three

colors like
a crushed
peach

like spilled ketchup
dripping
from
the kitchen table

there's no
technique

no, not
really

each mistake's
a blessing
to go
another way

HITCHHIKER PROVERBS

elsewhere is the oldest place

***

when you walk
even as you look at your feet
remember the sky

***

the hummingbird
can fly backwards
still knows
where he is

***

a bed is not so comfortable
if you like the smell of a ditch

***

the bear eats where
he wants

***

regardless
how dirty the mirror
it sees both sides

***

when you tell yourself
a secret
there's an echo

GROWING UP WITHOUT WINGS

her mother told her

fear any man
whose voice
grows louder in the dark
he is not the one
to marry

but if
for too many days
the brown of his eyes reminds you
of a forest
to hide in

if saying yes ever seems
not only
the easiest
but
the only path

then keep your voice down
on the phone

learn to keep quiet secrets

also
keep a few dollars
hidden
maybe wrapped in an old sweater's wool warmth
maybe in an empty makeup case
places a man will never search

will never think to

keep at least
one friend
from before your marriage
who knows you
by your scraped knee stories
by the deep chest sounds of your laugh
this friend will be
an island
in a river that changes course

more than all this
remember
even if you pray and pray nightly
with full belief and unfisted heart
prayer only works
outside the reach of his arms

JAILBIRD

some people belong in prison
my mother
said
about my father
who after fifty-two years on earth
left behind
three milk crates of possessions
and a rented room
high cherokee cheekbones
a love of white wine and the old testament
and a dance called the "prison shuffle"
mom would
never do

sit down
she would say
when i tried to get her
to dance

when i was with your father
i had enough dancing
to do me
until cows or jesus
came home

she always
laughed
when she said that
as if she were saying it
for the first time

EAST OF ELIZABETH CITY

one night a wave
came along
lifted a fellow
off our ship's
stern

hours passed
until he
was
missed

first light
barely
a promise

half the crew
came on deck
to scan waves

captain
circled back

two hours in
we came
to him

lips blue, teeth
chattering

in one hand
a shoe
held tight as
any wish

took a while
to get him
to let go

said he'd seen
sharks circle
big as him

that dolphins
chased them off

pushed him up
each time he
went under

told the story
again and
again

blessed cork
dark water

LISTENING TO AN OLD FRIEND TALK,
ON A PENNSYLVANIA HILLSIDE, LATE AUTUMN

I.

the wind on the hill grass
same as the wind on the river
same as the wind in my hair grown long with
        the season

the wind surprises us
seems to come from nowhere
across field, water, and sky

middle age and old age, both surprise us
along a dirt path, suddenly, a vast rock pile of
        years

II.

i've forgotten some of my words
some of the long, precise, melodious ones
used for crossword puzzles
not for singing

i can only speak simply now
i can make little comments about the weather

winter is coming
the air already settling with a chill

BLUES FOR GENE,
WHO WAS ALMOST FICTIONAL

he loved three wives
until he didn't
left broken hearts and bar tabs
but no children

also loved crown whisky (straight)
and his red, vintage, rebuilt truck

spent time in the navy
to pursue other interests
he would say
then laugh and cough and laugh

his shadow large
like a doorframe
no matter the day
or the sun

never drove slow in any car
no, not once
of course, never counted
calories

after brief illness
told a friend
enough of this
then drove away

gave himself
a birthday bullet
in the mouth

same friend found him
the next day

his large body
already tired at forty

OFF INTERSTATE 95

a good town to get your nails done in
or pawn a guitar

it's a place for stop signs and exits

people hope for jury duty
'cause it's a job

in the civil war sherman just rode past
burned nothing
a little fact the locals still mention

if you are young and spend the night
in the motel
you'll dream you are old

in the morning that dream won't linger
like a heat wave over the road

a long way back dreams learned to go

LETTER TO THE TOWN TOURIST BUREAU

a hole appeared in the church roof
last summer

now, it's spring

a worn blue tarp covers
bright against faded shingles

the church, still worth more
than most houses here

parishioners finger the collection plate
lust for any newness
(clothes and toys in their first season)

town bar gave up credit
when promises
became favored currency

wind blows down daily from the hills
the silted river smells second hand

III.

"Once people slept in gardens.
Now note even photography
can get you out of prison."
— Ira Cohen

Twenty Years In, Still Trying to Meditate

nothing happens
then it happens again

a fly buzzes on one side of the window
wind blows against the other side

a car passes
then a motorcyle

the fly stops
or moves on

open my eyes
there's sunlight

close them again
it's still there

NAVIGATING IN PLACE

we are always looking down

true, above us, clouds take the shape we wish
and there seems no end to the sky's depth of
        blue

but it's what's right beneath our feet
that holds attention

we find a rock, a piece of trash, a bone-shaped
        stick
we can't look away from

we fall in love with the misshapen, with cast off
        things
we build a life from the architecture of debris

our stories start in the dirt and go up or down
        from there
this is even true of the fairy tales where every
        creature has wings

TALKING WITH ALLEN GINSBERG, IN A DREAM

i'm in ginsberg's apartment
he sips tea
from a ceramic cup with no handle
looks thoughtful in a white, cotton kimono
that's a little stained, a little frayed at sleeves
the kimono's half open
shows gray hairs above a
wrinkled, pot belly
as he leans against his small kitchen counter
not a "cooker's kitchen"
instead a place to heat canned soup
make sandwiches
eat late night yogurt and veggie snacks

i tell him
my favorite of your books
is the last one
death and fame

you like posthumous things
he asks
cause i do...always have...even now

i tell him
it's mainly that last poem
the one about your funeral
i love those
jokey lines

i'll show you how i do it
he says
(starts to sway back and forth)
begin slowly or quickly
clear your mind
let one thought bleed to another
this can take a while
maybe an hour or twelve
that last poem was good
could have been bad
too often are
that's ok
turn bad poems into paper airplanes
bless them and toss

AMERICA

lately, you seem smaller
no longer with a capital letter in your name
your large A has run off with Apple stocks and
      Avon
you are the size of a field mouse
i can fit you into my shirt pocket
i can carry you to the mailbox, to the barn, to
the grocery store when i go
to get my bread and radishes
your squeak needs a megaphone to sound like a
      roar
i can scratch your ears and your head, but you
      keep biting my fingers
america, you can learn to walk on a leash, it's
      not so bad
ask the housecat, ask the badger
your tricks no different than the circus lion in
      his ring
only a bright and shiny thimble to stand on
      instead of chair

SINCE YOU LEFT

my clothes
don't match the way
painters and sunday
school teachers
say they should
a friend told me
it looks like you've
given up trying
i know what
he meant, but
he's wrong
truth is, lately,
i hardly think of clothes
i'm more concerned
with my garden
and all i didn't plant
this spring
true, there are peppers,
both hot and bell,
and cucumbers,
zuchinnis,
and enough
tomatoes to keep
the squirrels
happy in their
pillage
there's even a
little basil,
a little dill
i've never planted
flowers in my garden,

beside vegetables
and herbs, i've not
planted them
beside the
porch steps
or mailbox
there are none
anywhere in
my yard
they serve
no purpose
but beauty
i thought
nothing lines
the driveway
but grass and a
few, large festive
painted rocks
you left for me
to pick up,
not toss

CROW FACTS & VARIATIONS

if god were a crow
the world would spin in the black pearl of her eyes

the world would spin and spin
black would be the color to measure others by

***

if crows could reach the stars
they would

they'd have new worlds to scavenge among

crows are scavengers
(read survivors)

crows make do

***

a field crow calls out in that broken voice
not even a crow mother loves

crows can nest in silence
if they must

Maker of Bicycles & What-Not

howard
ate instant coffee grounds
with a spoon
right from the jar

so little time for niceties
so much to be quickly done

we wondered
if everything
was a rush

if his five children
were all conceived
on the way to the next thing

BRANDO IN TAHITI

let's say it's late
past midnight

beach nearly empty
except for stray,
exhausted
lovers
and brando
in beach towel,
sandals

he tends a fire
so close to
the tide
logs sizzle
with mist

now and then
a spark floats
towards sky

stars so
numerous
even the
smallest hand
could block
a dozen
from view

every few minutes
brando
        (who
seems as large
as the island,
his great yell
louder than
a bullhorn)
        throws pages
into the fire
from a stack
of scripts
beside him

the fire grows
brighter as
the stack grows
smaller

brando drinks
from a wine jug
impersonates
pacino and laughs
laughs, laughs

Tu Fu, in Exile, in Middle Age

calm lake a mirror to the mountains
at the center a fisherman's boat rests

tu fu, so long away from the capital,
envies the fisherman and his net

wife crying in another room
not a bowl of rice in the house

not one persimmon for the children
of course, no wine for late hours alone

he wishes for a gift or a letter
drinks water from his gourd cup

the mountains are large, but no closer,
that fisherman always works alone

SHORT POEMS
for Michael Wurster

i love short poems

i love the how of what they do
a continent of breath in three or four or nine lines
a comma along the water
an asterisk in sand

LOSING VERBS

years provide losses

your body
no longer uses
words
like *run*
like *trot*, even

you no longer think
to climb stairs
so suddenly steep
they ascend to
heaven's
far side

sex, of course, of course
moves, one last time,
from act
to thought

you become like
a middle-school boy
dreaming
what's beneath
summer dresses

WHAT I KNOW ABOUT POETRY
for Geraldine Cannon

some things keep happening

a rock rolls down a hill, bounces, bounces, rolls
       along
makes a sound every time it bumps the dirt

the rock rolls until it doesn't
until it finds a ditch
a small rock pile

over time, the ditch might fill up
the rock pile might make a mountain
the cracks stay

IV.

"the inner birds singing
alone in this house that I love"
—James Tate

YOU MAKE ME FEEL

like a dog with the face of a rhino, like a rhino
with the colors of a peacock, like a peacock with
the attitude of a house cat, like a house cat with
the speed of a sloth, like a sloth with the language
of a sailor, like a sailor with the magic of a fairy,
like a fairy with a coke habit, like a fairy with a
coke habit, like a coke habit with a coke habit

MARRIAGE SUITE

i can make nothing
with my hands

have learned
no craft
of wood, needle
or stone

am often wrong on
measurements

all i know of
geometry
comes from studying
the lines
of your face

***

some things i know
only from
you

are true because
you said them

whole world might
say otherwise

***

i watch your hands
in the quiet canyon of your sleep
there are dreams you
follow
again and again

they are the stories you tell
on waking

***

dreams are the second best thing
you always
say

you've always said

***

after these many years
memory takes up
more space

once, it used just a closet
now, it demands a whole floor

***

that first, rented house
with barely a bed and table

one neighbor came
with green apples
and water
in a clear, glass jar

she sat with us
told us
how it was
before we came

THE NIGHT AFTER YOU LEFT,
I DREAMED THE WHOLE WORLD WAS BURNING

woke to the sound
of rain
on the roof

all night the dream
of fire

       house
       fields around house
       woods to town's edge
       town and townspeople

also birds
strange flightless birds
(red, black and black)

all the birds
calling, calling

did eve's lips
grow lustful
after the first
bite of the
apple did she
inhale in
anticipation
of adam's
scent think
of her own
which she
barely knew
did she
quickly look
over each
shoulder to
see if the
animals saw
her different
before she
even chewed

The Very Beginning, and After

your mother wished and wished
for a girl

dressed you as one
first three years of your life, her sorrow

many years since you've been re-reading the print
lace left on your skin

goldfish remember nothing
long enough to mourn

you remember
almost everything

pink easter dress in a picnic field
how she called you *princess, princess*

sky's open eggshell of spring clouds
that world without end

1978

my grandmother burned her outhouse down
insisted, at last, on indoor plumbing

my brother quit high school, amid my
father's curses and my mother's sighs,

joined the navy which sent him nowhere
more exotic than california in his three years

uncle mason finished building his fishing boat
used scrap lumber (called it crap lumber)

a heart attack took him the next summer
aunt virginia left the boat to rats and squirrels

around the world jim jones led the guyana mess
also a new pope came and left, quickly, in rome

i learned how to peddle my bike downhill
saw *superman* three times with my then best friend

MY PARENTS

1.
the horizon is my father
back from the sea
       his eyes
shallow blue

they are blue
because i see them, know they are blue
they are blue because
he tells me his eyes are what people
(read women/girls)
notice first

       beach sky blue
       vacation blue
       dixie-land trumpet blue
       not blue like *the blues*
       blue with no shadow sadness

2.
my mother left one day
in her small, white car
to get groceries

never came back

her eyes
almost green
       (red in the corners)

       when she squinted
       they took the shape of wings

AT THE END OF THINGS

our bodies fall away from us
our shadows turn upside down
our shadows make a bed for us

In the Country of Grief

as though you are ill
on a journey

hands filled with
absences

mouth with a thousand
raw questions

the taste of sand

Marriage Proposal: A Found Poem

free estimate
available

inventory includes
socks, shoes, books, kitchen utensils, toothpaste
        tubes,
headaches, hard laughs, affection nearly always,
sickness real and imagined,
gravity induced wrinkles and frowns

all this
done
at your home
while
you wait

no pressure
sale limited
no lifetime guarantee

THE CROWS

i love those damned birds
for what they aren't

lovely, dainty
beloved

also, for what
they are

scrappy, clever
unafraid of stick men

the crow knows his
only world

his knowledge
complete

he carries a spine
of darkness

his home, some place
i never see

DREAM OF DEATH AND THE PLANE RIDE THERE

i look around to check for crowds
but soon realize the lone white jet is just for me

the only other person on the tarmac is a man
who looks both official and unremarkable

i'm sure i've met him and forgotten

the man says nothing, but motions for me to
        "move it along"
as though he has somewhere else to be

on board, there's no flight attendant
i am the only passenger and there's no assigned
        seating

no voice comes over the intercom as the plane
        door closes
no one reminds me to buckle up

after a while, sure enough, i am flying
up and away i go

MANY HAPPY RETURNS
for Diane

i don't believe in reincarnation
but if it happens
if i get a return trip
i'll find you
though i may have a different size or shape

i might be the crow you can't scare from the
            garden
i might be the mouse that dodges every trap you
            set

Carrboro, North Carolina, November

the town is like a woman, ripe with love
that sounds like autumn,
so it is

all the unnecessaries
falling way
the world left to essentials

restaurant patio furniture
stored for winter

sidewalks washed to a deeper grey

even the skinny, skinny woman
bivouacked on the corner
north of
the coffee shop
even she is calling it quits

her violin brings fewer tips with the cold
her needs more than weather

Late Rothko

what's within a square
stays

> *light*
> *darkness*

a closed world
perfect or not

some places we can't go
no matter our tools or instruments

so we give up knowing
and give up knowing

no light gets through
no colors

no reds, no oranges
no whites

WHY I MEDITATE
after Anne Waldman

i sit because there's no anger in this pose
i sit because no one ever told me not to
i sit because others, smarter, sat before me
i sit because in my wallet, right now, $11.83,
        two credit cards (one expired), a receipt
        for a bagel and a past due dental notice
i sit to follow my breath wherever it goes
i sit because i have children, so might be an
        example to them as they to me
i sit for the joy of sitting
i sit because i'm silly like that
i sit for a sometimes knowledge of grace
i sit to laugh at myself, all that i do, don't do
i sit because it's better than most television, many
        movies
i sit because sitting gathers my world to me while
i stay in one place
i sit because in junk shop statues the buddha
        looks happy
i sit to calm my crazy darkness, embrace absence
        too
i sit because it empties me like a cup waiting to
        be filled

POSTCARD INVITATION FROM NEW LODGINGS

our house is far enough outside of town
to almost be a destination

a star map or a compass
can, just about, lead you here

i tell every friend
if you are near, stop by

let me see how your shadow hangs to your body
let me know your hands are still warm

A Photograph of W.S. Merwin

a half-smile on
his lips

as if the very
thought of speech
is pleasure

light through the window
behind him

green light on leaves
light on distant hills

no sign of rain

left hand beginning
to rise
gesture in the air to beckon

MY FATHER COULD

tell stories
so miraculous

their veracity
could not
be trusted
but so funny
so goddamn
funny
you thought
for a clear
second
the world was
that place
where
happiness
came easy —
stayed —
you forgot
holding joy
longer
than a
moment
is as difficult
as licking
honey
off a rusty
razor blade

ABOUT THE AUTHOR

Mike James was born in the red clay hills of South Carolina and grew up amid tobacco, cotton fields and closing textile mills. He received his BA from Winthrop University and his MA from Duquesne University.

His poems have appeared in numerous magazines throughout the country in such places as *Birmingham Poetry Review*, *5 AM*, *Negative Capability*, and *Chiron Review*. Among his ten previous poetry collections are *My Favorite Houseguest* (Futurecyle, 2017), *Peddler's Blues* (Main Sreet Rag, 2016), and *Past Due Notices: Poems 1991-2011* (Main Street Rag, 2012).

He served as an associate editor at both *The Kentucky Review* and Autumn House Press, as the publisher of Yellow Pepper Press, and as the Waneta T. Blake Visiting Professor at the University of Maine, Fort Kent.

After years spent in Missouri, Pennsylvania, and Georgia, he now makes his home in Chapel Hill, North Carolina with his large family and a large assortment of cats.

BOOKS BY BOTTOM DOG PRESS

HARMONY SERIES

Crows in the Jukebox: Poems, by Mike James, 106 pgs., $16

Portrait of the Artist as a Bingo Worker, by Lori Jakiela, 216 pgs, $18

The Thick of Thin by Larry Smith, 238 pgs, $18

Cold Air Return by Patrick Lawrence O'Keeffe, 390 pgs, $20

Flesh and Stones: Field Notes from a Finite World by Jan Shoemaker, 176 pgs, $18

Waiting to Begin: A Memoir by Patricia O'Donnell, 166 pgs. $18

And Waking: Poems by Kevin Casey, 80 pgs, $16

Both Shoes Off: Poems by Jeanne Bryner, 112 pgs, $16

Abandoned Homeland: Poems by Jeff Gundy, 96 pgs. $16

Stolen Child: A Novel by Suzanne Kelly, 338 pgs. $18

The Canary : A Novel by Michael Loyd Gray, 196 pgs. $18

On the Flyleaf: Poems by Herbert Woodward Martin, 106 pgs. $16

The Harmonist at Nightfall: Poems of Indiana by Shari Wagner, $16

Painting Bridges: A Novel by Patricia Averbach, 234 pgs. $18

Ariadne & Other Poems by Ingrid Swanberg, 120 pgs. $16

The Search for the Reason Why: New and Selected Poems by Tom Kryss, 192 pgs. $16

Kenneth Patchen: Rebel Poet in America by Larry Smith, Revised 2nd Edition, 326 pgs. Cloth $28

Selected Correspondence of Kenneth Patchen, Edited with introduction by Allen Frost, Paper $18/ Cloth $28

Awash with Roses: Collected Love Poems of Kenneth Patchen Eds. Laura Smith and Larry Smith With introduction by Larry Smith, 200 pgs. $16

Breathing the West: Great Basin Poems by Liane Ellison Norman, $16

Maggot : A Novel by Robert Flanagan, 262 pgs. $18

American Poet: A Novel by Jeff Vande Zande, 200 pgs. $18

The Way-Back Room: Memoir of a Detroit Childhood by Mary Minock, 216 pgs. $18

www.ingramcontent.com/pod-product-compliance
Lightning Source LLC
Chambersburg PA
CBHW031143090426
42738CB00008B/1200